Online Trading and Stock Investing for Beginners

Baby Beginners *Presents*

Online Trading and Stock Investing for Beginners

The Easy Way to Start Trading and Getting Rich in the Stock Market

Michael Wells & Instafo

instafo

Copyright © Instafo

All rights reserved.

It is impermissible to reproduce any part of this book without prior consent. All violations will be prosecuted to the fullest extent of the law.

While attempts have been made to verify the information contained within this publication, neither the author nor the publisher assumes any responsibility for errors, omissions, interpretation or usage of the subject matter herein.

This publication contains the opinions and ideas of its author and is intended for informational purpose only. The author and publisher shall in no event be held liable for any loss or other damages incurred from the usage of this publication.

ISBN 978-1-691-32708-9

Printed in the United States of America

First Edition

Table of Contents

Chapter 1: The Mandatory New Approach for Money Management

1.1 The Slow Death of Money..11

1.2 Big Reasons to Invest..14

1.3 Types of Financial Investments..................................17

1.4 The Preferable Option...22

1.5 Advantageous Variety...23

1.6 Convenient Liquidity..27

1.7 Profitable Volatility...28

1.8 To-Do: Saving Vs. Investing.......................................29

Chapter 2: Generating Cumulative Wealth through Investing

2.1 The Power of Dividend Reinvesting..........................31

2.2 Exponential Growth through the Compounding Effect..35

2.3 A Passive Income Stream with Dividend..................38

Chapter 3: Getting and Using the Tools of the Stock Trader

3.1 Trading Platforms..42

3.2 Stock Brokerages..44

3.3 Robo-Advisors..48

3.4 To-Do: Find Your Broker...51

Chapter 4: Building the Foundational Core Understanding

4.1 Starting from the Basic...53

4.2 The Mechanism of the Market....................................55

4.3 Investor Hierarchy Levels..56

4.4 To-Do: Solidify Investment Goal................................59

Chapter 5: Controlling and Mastering the Stock Market

5.1 Honing an Investor's Intuition....................................60

5.2 The Driving Polar Forces of the Market....................63

5.3 The Art of Stock Analysis..68

5.4 The Candlestick Chart..71

5.5 The Trendlines Chart..74

5.6 The ABCD Chart..75

5.7 Common Trading Terms..77
5.8 To-Do: Rubber Meets the Road................................79

Chapter 6: Taking Action and Initiating the Trading Process

6.1 Choosing Companies for Personal Portfolio..............81
6.2 Steps to Practice Risk Management..........................84
6.3 To-Do: Calculate Risk Benchmarks..........................88
6.4 Cumulative Overview: Five-Action Steps to Take Now!..90

Chapter 7: The Prosperous Final Outlook for Financial Future

7.1 A Renewed Financial Affair.....................................101
7.2 Fear Not the Loss of Money but of Time................103

*DISCLAIMER:

Please firmly keep in mind that there is no guarantee that you will ever make any money at all from the stock market – but in fact incur losses. Many factors will vary actual results, including and not limited to uncontrollable ones. Any type of investing is always risky, and you should proceed at your own risk.

Chapter 1:

The Mandatory New Approach for Money Management

The Slow Death of Money

The *shrinking* middle class and growing financial hurdles, particularly **inflation,** have made sure that our salaries alone are no longer enough to provide a comfortable life for ourselves and our families.

People go to school with the goal of learning things and eventually getting a job that will earn them money. Yet, due to the imperfect economic systems, people are rarely self-sufficient, leading to a growth in the culture of dependency. They depend on the government for health, housing, retirement, and more. This rat race of earning to pay off debt continues, for some, until death. This also highlights how much our educational system neglects the importance of teaching people *how to make money*.

On the other hand, some people make much more than others even without a fancy education. This means that wealth is not dependent on your academic qualifications but rather on how much knowledge you can garner on the topic of **wealth creation**.

In the past, financial experts said people should *save* a good portion of their job earnings in order to create wealth. But the twists and turns in the economy over the past three decades have rendered that "saving" idea obsolete. Sure, saved money grows nominally, but that has no use for the typical saver. Many people wind up having to work longer hours or second jobs just to stay on top of their bills while trying to secure their financial future.

Now, the modern idea promoted by economic experts is the need to *invest extra money* so that it can yield a reasonable amount which will augment the earnings from your day job. Investing your earnings is a way of doubling or even tripling them.

One popular option is **trading in the stock market**. Unlike regular jobs, stock trading surprisingly requires a minimal amount of your time and can bring about a geometric growth of your money *passively*. Furthermore, all you need is a computer, tablet, or smartphone with internet access, along with a good platform to begin trading in stocks.

We all dream of making lots of money. But dreams alone do not create wealth. Determination and hard or smart work do. For a beginner, it can be daunting trying to navigate through and figure out the stock market. Fear not, for we shall guide you on how to master the craft of trading in stocks starting from square one.

Big Reasons to Invest

People used to believe that the best way to become rich was by *living below your means* and *saving what's left*. However, with a good investment, you don't have to live like a pauper, and your savings will still grow. Investing is a better option than saving for a number of reasons.

Firstly and pivotally, it has a tremendous **compound effect**.

> In the "Parable of the Talents" in the Bible, a master left his servants in charge of his property when he departed for a trip. On his way out, the master gave one servant five talents, another two talents, and the third he gave one talent. (A "talent" represented a significant amount of money.)
>
> When the master finally returned, he asked his servants what they did with his money. The first servant invested his five talents and earned five more. The

second servant also invested and doubled his talents from two to four. However, the third servant hid his one talent and then returned it to the master when he got back.

The master rewarded the two servants who invested and multiplied his wealth, and he punished the third servant for simply saving the money and not earning anything.

As you can see, even the Bible recognizes the importance of investing over saving.

Economists say saved money *loses its value* to **inflation** over time. Here's a hypothetical example.

Let's say you saved $1,000 in 1990, which was more than enough to pay your rent or your monthly car payment. Living that same lifestyle with the mentality of saving over investing would be extremely difficult now. However, if you had invested that $1,000 wisely in 1990, it could have been worth more than $100,000 by now.

While we're advocating how much better it is to invest rather than save, you may be wondering why so many banks try to get customers to open savings accounts. *The answer is simple.* The banks want your money so they can invest it and make profits for themselves.

A typical savings account has an **interest rate** of less than 1%. So once you hand over some money to the bank and make very little interest, they'll give out your money as a loan to someone else with an interest rate as high as 10-15%.

- Bottom Line: You make very little money, and the bank makes a lot!

People who still prefer saving over investing will argue that *investing is risky*. Yes, everything in life, including life itself, carries some level of risk. But what's far riskier than investing is **financial illiteracy**. Investment is a *calculated risk* in financial management. However, you can lower that risk with sufficient planning and knowledge of what you are going into.

Types of Financial Investments

Let's say you have a dog or a cat as a pet. If someone invited you to go with them to the zoo, you wouldn't say *"no"* simply because you already have an animal to look at in your own home.

Financial investments are the same way. There are many investment options. Just because you may already invest in one doesn't mean you shouldn't take a look at the others. You never want to miss out on other opportunities for financial growth.

Seeing the features of the different investment options will help you to decide whether to stick with what you are doing or make some changes. Here are a few choices:

a.) **Bonds** - This is a kind of loan that an investor makes to an organization or the government. There is an agreement that the money will be paid back with interest at the end of a stipulated time. This is a very safe investment, but the reward is typically smaller and the organization's success will also affect your payback time and your perceived interest.

b.) **Mutual funds** - This is a pooling of finances by many investors to buy diversified investments. It is usually managed by a group of financial professionals. So instead of investing in a bunch of individual stocks on your own, a mutual fund lets the experts pick a group of stocks for you. To buy and sell a mutual fund, you'd have to do so through the group managing it. A mutual fund is like an old-school grandfather's way of buying diversified stocks and is becoming more unnecessary (not to mention the hefty management fees) due to newer and better fund options like **index funds** and **exchange-traded funds**.

c.) **Real estate** - Real estate needs no introduction. It is an investment in housing. Real estate ranges from renting, building, and selling properties, as well as helping people locate a place to live for themselves.

d.) **Stock market** - Here, an investor buys a part of a company. When a company is doing well and plans to expand but has less capital than what is required for the expansion, it invites the public to invest in it by a process called an "**initial public offering (IPO)**." It will divide the capital needs into little fractions called "**shares**." The shares can then be bought by the public or investors. Once you have shares with a company, you are an investor and a shareholder of the company. You are entitled to know how the company is faring and the **profit (dividend)** made by the company. You can reinvest the dividend to have more shares. You can also sell shares when you are in need of money.

e.) **Index funds** - This is a kind of investment similar to the stock market but it's a passive style of investing. An index fund allows a broad exposure of investments at a time in different companies *(Coca-Cola, Apple, Facebook, etc.)* or sectors *(finance, health care, renewable energy, etc.)* in order to minimize the losses which normally occur in investments.

The easy way to think of an index is like the **categories** *(types of companies or sectors)* listed in the index of a book, and then it has all its chosen **related sub-categories** below *(individual companies under those types or sectors).*

- S&P 500: The most important index that you should know is the **S&P 500**. The S&P 500 index, which was first created in 1923 by the financial company Standard & Poor's, has become the standard in measuring market performance. Companies in the United States are grouped based on their capitalization. Index funds for the S&P 500 index are for those top 500 companies with the highest monetary capital and are doing pretty well. Their activities heavily affect the stability of the market due to the fact that their capital has the greatest percentage in the stock market. *(*Remember the S&P 500 <u>now</u> because we will come back to this later on why the S&P 500 is probably the best route for any beginner investor to follow.)*

f.) **Exchange-traded funds (ETFs)** - This is very *similar to index funds* but **acts more like a stock** that can be bought or sold at any time open to the public, while an **index fund is more like a mutual fund** closed off to members only.

- For example, while the S&P 500 is a market index, there are ETFs that trade the same S&P 500 index fund – like the <u>VOO</u> (**Vanguard S&P 500 ETF**), <u>VTI</u> (**iShares Core S&P 500 ETF**), and <u>SPY</u> (**SPDR S&P 500**).

- Here's another way to look at it: *ETFs are the franchisees* and the *index fund is the franchise* offering its business model and menu items (their list of categorized companies or sectors) to the franchisee so they can operate it to the public (being the stock market) where anybody can now walk in and purchase items (in this case trade stocks).

If some of these terminologies are still confusing, don't worry too much about them. You'll naturally grasp them once you actually start investing.

The Preferable Option

Many of these investment options either require you to place your earnings on the shoulders of another entity or require a huge capital like in the case of real estate. That's why **investing in the stock market** is the preferable option.

Understandably, buying stock in *some* companies can be expensive too, but there are many progressive companies with low-cost stocks. You can start trading with as little as $50 to $100, depending on the platform.

Also, stock trading is an investment you can start on the go, as long as you understand the nitty-gritty. It's also flexible in the sense that you can trade from any part of the world as long as you have an internet-enabled smartphone or computer.

There are lots of reasons why you should prioritize stock investing over the other investment options which we will now explore.

Advantageous Variety

There are thousands of companies in which you can invest your money. This also gives you room to diversify your investment. But you don't *have* to invest in multiple companies. In most cases, one is enough.

For example, billionaire Warren Buffet did not know much about technology, but he knew very much about Coca-Cola. So he was comfortable with the company and got interested to the point that he decided to buy about $1 billion in Coke stock back in the late 1980s. Now, his shares are worth more than $16 billion.

The good thing about investing in stock is that you can find a company that has the qualities, flexibility, and specifications that you desire. In choosing to invest in stocks, you have to consider your age, income, and your financial plan.

You can decide to invest in **Value Appreciation Companies** or **Growth Companies**.

A Value Appreciation Company, also simply known as a **Dividend Company**, is a company that pays you part of its profit (dividend) based on the number of stocks you own in a specified time period.

Let's say that the company made $1 million as profit in a given year, and you own 10%. You will be paid $100,000 as *your dividend*. This type of investment is better suited for those close to retirement and those who will be needing bulk extra cash. A scenario is a man who would be retiring in the next five years. This type of investment is stable and risk-free since even a bear market cannot affect it deeply.

The other one is investing in **Growth Companies**.

For example, Ronald Wayne unconsciously chose not to be popular through his actions. He and his friends Steve Jobs and Steve Wozniak co-founded Apple Inc. in the 1970s.

Jobs and Wozniak were 25 and 21 years old, respectively. Wayne was in his 40s. When they started the company, Wayne drafted the founding document and logo of the company which was used for one year. But he left Apple because he did not believe in its survival and sustainability. He finally sold his shares which was 10% of the company for $800. *Big mistake!*

If he did not sell the shares, he would have been one of the richest men on earth. This story is a great lesson in *growth investing*. Basically, growth investing is when you invest in a company that shows significant signs that it will experience exceptional growth in value. This form of investment is best suited for the younger investors and risk-takers who are not in immediate need of money. In other words, it is an *ideal long-term investment*.

- <u>Dividend</u>: Having talked so much about dividend, it is important to reinforce a good comprehension of it. A dividend is essentially a "payout a company gives to its shareholders," typically *quarterly* but sometimes *monthly*, for investors' loyalty in sticking with them rather than selling their shares. Newly launched companies' dividend payouts are almost non-existent due to the growth potential in expansion, not to mention it is unlikely these baby companies will generate enough revenue (yet) to pay out dividends to all their investors. Older, established companies, on the other hand, don't have much room for growth; so to offset that, they offer dividends as incentives, plus they can afford to do so having been around for a while.

Convenient Liquidity

Imagine a man who has ten homes and decides to sell one. He would go to an agent who would give him a time frame in which he is likely to find a buyer. In most cases, the seller may be in need of money and will be forced to sell below the valued price.

But in the stock market, there is a ready market waiting to buy from you. Therefore, depending on the supply and demand curve, you are likely to sell at a higher price.

- Simply put, **liquidity** is how much *freedom* and *flexibility* you have turning that investment into cash.

With stocks, you can easily sell them at any time you want – so they have *high liquidity*. This contrasts to real estate that has *low liquidity* because you can't quickly sell a property and turn it into cash immediately. Instead, you have to wait and hopefully find a buyer first, which could take weeks, months, years, or maybe never. And once you do find a buyer, the process can take months to finalize the exchange.

Profitable Volatility

Volatility is the *rapid change in the price of equities* (**shares**).

Whenever you read about stock market shares, one of the recommendations is to buy a volatile stock if you're looking to do **day trading** – buying and selling stocks for the short term. Volatile stock is the kind of stock that has price changes over time.

> For example, a stock can move from $\underline{\$1.20}$ to $\underline{\$1.30}$ during the *day* or even move to $\underline{\$2.50}$ in a *week*. This is unlike in real estate where the price changes only *after a long period of time*. Moreover, the price change of stocks does not affect the market stability of the company involved. It is only as a result of **supply and demand**.

The movement of prices of stock in the market does not necessarily mean anything as long as it is not caused by the management of the company.

To-Do: Saving Vs. Investing

Still not convinced whether you should be in the stock market? Then this exercise will help you understand the advantage of **investing** *over* **saving**:

1. Save $\underline{\$100}$ in your **bank account** for three-to-six months without touching it.

2. Invest $\underline{\$100}$ using a **micro-investment app** (Popular options include Acorns, Stash, and Robinhood.). Although many of the micro-investment apps will allow you to invest *as little as* $\underline{\$5}$, try and invest up to $\underline{\$100}$ to keep things even. Just like with your savings in the first step, leave your stock investment alone for three-to-six months.

3. At the end of that waiting period, compare the interest generated by your savings account and your micro-investment. *Which is higher?*

4. Now divide the interest by three-to-six months – depending on how long you invested. This gives you an idea of the average of what your savings or investment earned you in a month. You can multiply this figure by $\underline{60}$ (60 months total) to see what you would expect in five years. *Which is higher?*

Chapter 2:

Generating Cumulative Wealth through Investing

The Power of Dividend Reinvesting

A priest was asked when is the best time to plant a tree. He said, *"The best time is twenty years ago. Nevertheless, another time is now."* That answer most definitely applies to stocks too. That's because investments appreciate with time.

The major reason why you need to start investing now is to leverage the power of **dividend reinvesting**. Dividend reinvesting means that the dividends you earn are reinvested back into the stock. So basically, you use your dividends to buy more shares of the same stock.

- For example, let's pretend you own a 1% share in a company, and you earn a $250 dividend each quarter for a total of $1,000 dividend at the end of the 12-month year. *The kicker?* Reinvesting each of the four $250 dividend payments means you will own an even larger share – and earn a larger dividend than $1000 – at the end of the next year. And the growth will be even bigger and bigger each year because you'll have more shares.

Why would you want to do this? That is because of the **"compounding effect"** that comes from investing over time.

EX:
$250 quarterly dividend non-reinvested (or withdrawn) by the end of the year = $1,000

VS.

$250 quarterly dividend reinvested on top of the previous amount with a 10% return *(just to keep the math simple)* to exemplify the compounding effect

(First $250 Dividend) = $250
(Second $250 Dividend + $250 Reinvested) x 0.10 = $50 + ($500) = $550
(Third $250 Dividend + $550 Reinvested) x 0.10 = $80 + ($800) = $880
(Fourth $250 Dividend + $880 Reinvested) x 0.10 = $113 + ($1,130) = $1,243

Notice the sum difference in reinvesting each $250 dividend over NOT investing it or withdrawing that amount as cash quarterly, you will get **$1,243** instead of the **$1,000** after 12 months all thanks to the compounding effect. (Side-Note: If you did get a 10% return that did *NOT* compound quarterly you would still have gotten a lesser amount of **$1,100** at the end of the year, so compounding your amount as frequently as possible is what you want.)

- This can be done manually, or set up automatically each time a dividend is paid out with the "**dividend reinvestment plan (DRIP)**" at your brokerage.

Following this path could make you wealthy, and it will also give you a significant stake in the company as well as increase your relevance. Who knows, maybe one day you'll become a board member.

As a rule of thumb, investing at least 10% of your earnings is what can increase your wealth over time. If you have stock in a company and continue to invest in that stock even while your initial stock grows, the rest of the story is predictable. *"Show me the money!"*

Exponential Growth through the Compounding Effect

Now let's see what the compounding effect would look like in a real-life scenario.

If you invested $5,500 into a Roth IRA at age 40, and then invest an additional $5,500 each year for 20 years, you would be sitting on a nice pile of cash in time for retirement.

Assuming an average 10% return on investment each year, after 20 years, your investment would be worth more than $300,000.

Check out the results from the compound interest calculator at **NerdWallet** (www.nerdwallet.com/banking/calculator/compound-interest-calculator):

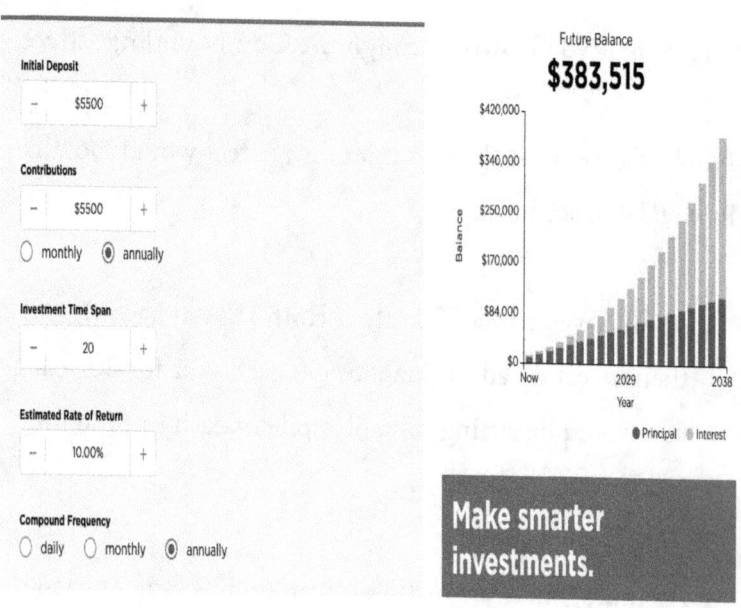

And remember, that's only a 20-year investment span. What if you did the same thing by starting at age 20? After 40 years, you'd have about $3 million in time for retirement!

Here's the updated chart:

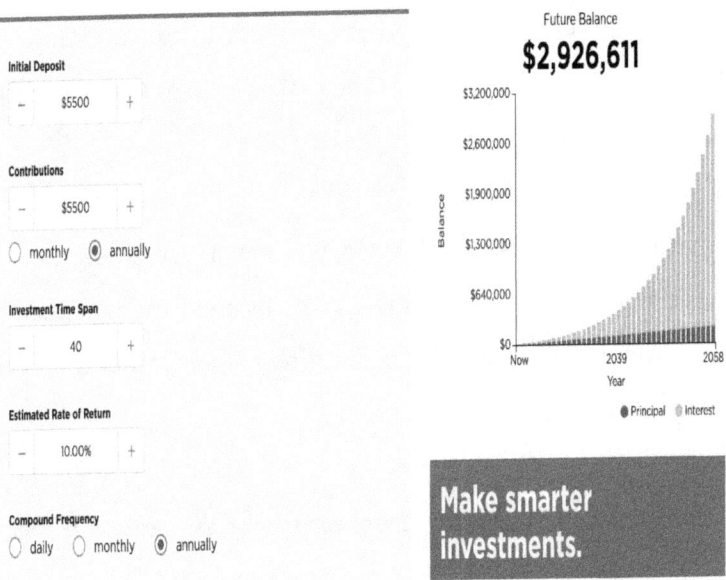

- Notice the exponential growth and how much steeper the chart becomes as time goes by. Time literally is free money when it comes to compounding.

Imagine becoming a multi-millionaire by the time you retire without having to do any extra work but just allowing the power of time to compound your earnings. Investing like this for the long term is the easiest way to grow wealth and become rich.

If you stick to this wealth cycle, you may be surprised at how much your net worth will grow by the time you need the money the most. This is definitely a goldmine to wealth that you cannot afford to ignore.

"Compound interest is the eighth wonder of the world. He who understands it, earns it...he who doesn't...pays it."
– **Albert Einstein**

A Passive Income Stream with Dividend

One last lucrative attraction about dividend investing is that you can actually live off of those stocks that pay you dividends *without* ever having to sell them.

When you retire or whenever you just decide to *no longer* reinvest your dividends, but rather withdraw them as spending money – it's possible to live comfortably from your dividends alone.

For example, if Microsoft pays around a $0.50 **dividend per share** and you own 100 shares, you'll get $500 **every three months** as passive income.

- Let's say Microsoft's shares cost $100 each, and you have $1 million to invest in them. That will give you 10,000 shares of Microsoft and a $5,000 payment every quarter (or about a **$1,700 monthly passive income**) – while *still owning* all your **10,000 shares of Microsoft,** which, of course, you can *sell at any time* to earn additional profit through the years that the stock price appreciates.

- Now let's amp this up a notch and say you're a billionaire. $1 billion will give you **10 million**

Microsoft shares and a quarterly dividend income of $5 million – or roughly **$1.7 million in monthly passive income!** You'll basically never have to work again and still be able to live a luxurious lifestyle. (For those of you in or thinking about real estate – no property maintenance and annoying hostile tenants to deal with.)

And do you wonder why the rich keep getting richer? That is because they already have enough money to let their money work for them to generate astronomically more.

Feeling excited (and maybe even a little secretly jealous)? Are you more convinced than ever as to why investing your money is better than saving it in a bank? Think of it like almost putting your money in a bank getting a higher-yield interest in the form of a dividend, yet on top of that with the added bonus of your money growing through appreciation over time – not to mention if you take advantage of the powerful compounding effect.

There's absolutely no competition! But remember, never put all of your eggs in one basket and always calculate and consider the risk.

Chapter 3:

Getting and Using the Tools of the Stock Trader

Trading Platforms

Any successful plan can be easily accomplished with the right tools. That said, it is important to expand your knowledge on stock trading by first knowing about the best platforms for trading stocks.

For stock trading, you will need a good software platform that allows you to buy and sell, and features cutting edge technologies that will help put you on a path to success. It's good to use one that has both **web** and **mobile** versions.

- The mobile app will allow you to make trades from anywhere. Just keep in mind that the full web versions are usually better than the mobile ones because they have more robust features.

There are many types of platforms set up by **brokerages**. *We'll explain brokerages in more detail in just a moment.*

But the first thing you should do when researching brokerages is make sure they are backed by the **Securities Investor Protection Corporation (SIPC)** so you'll be protected if your brokerage goes belly up due to corruption or fraud. For more information about **SIPC** and to check if a brokerage is a part of it, visit www.sipc.org/list-of-members.

Stock Brokerages

Brokerages are licensed and regulated financial firms that facilitate stock market trades. They are managed by **stockbrokers**.

Stockbrokers must have had some financial educational background such as accounting, marketing, or business. With the proper education, stockbrokers are in a better position to advise you on trades. Their functions are essential, especially when you are in need of financial advice. There are different types of brokers:

Full-Service Brokers: These brokers offer full service such as advice, which gives investors essential information on the stock market. They are ready to serve any potential investor. Most brokerages offer all full-service brokers. You can meet them in their offices for face-to-face human interaction, and they are available to help you whenever you need them.

Discount Service: This type of brokerage is the same as full service except in the allocation of time. Their brokers will provide you with service, but at a much lower level of customer engagement and availability.

Renowned brokerages include E*Trade, Vanguard, Charles Schwab, Robinhood, Fidelity, and Ameritrade.

The reason you would hire a stockbroker is, of course, to provide expertise and help you make money. And stockbrokers want to make money just as much as you do. Here are some of the ways they make a living.

a.) **Commission** - This is the main source of stockbrokers' livelihood, although some do not work on commission. Commission is the fee paid by investors for transactions. There are two types of commission:

- Per share: The investor pays a commission of a specific amount (sometimes around $0.004) for every share purchased or sold.

- Per trade: Here the investor pays a fixed price (such as $4.95) for the whole shares being bought or sold.

Neither of these methods of commission payment is better than the other. It depends largely on how much stock you buy. For example, if an investor wants to buy 700 shares of Microsoft stock, he should first calculate the two commission methods using the example prices above. For **per-share commission**, he would pay the broker $2.80 ($0.004 x 700). For **per-trade commission**, he would pay $4.95, which is approximately double the price per share. Obviously, you should pick the method that *saves you the most money*.

b.) **Funding and withdrawing from the account** - Before you begin trading in stocks, you will be required to fund your account. Some platforms charge a small amount on any money that comes into or out of the account.

c.) **Locate** - This is for a practice known as "short selling" – or *shorting a stock* as a way of making money when stock prices go down or speculating they will go down. *How?* Essentially, you borrow shares of a company from an existing owner through your broker. With shorting, you can sell first without having to buy first. Then you sell those borrowed shares at the current market price and keep the profit after having to buy them back at a lower price because remember, you're borrowing and will have to give the shares back eventually. A locate is the approval and process done by your broker prior to effecting a short sale. Your broker will charge you a fee for this.

Other ways in which brokers get money are **inactivity fees** and **platform fees,** *etc.* Sadly, some brokers only advise their clients in such a way only to get money for themselves.

This is especially the case where the new investor is perceived to be a novice in the stock market. Some brokers will divide their focus between helping you achieve your investment goals with helping to keep themselves in business and earning money.

Robo-Advisors

Robo-advisors are a type of financial advisor service that involves very little human interaction. Rather than relying on a human advisor who may not know all the important things to ask or say when providing financial services, robo-advisors provide advice based on mathematical rules and algorithms. In other words, you get your advice from software rather than a human.

How it works is you fill out a questionnaire or survey of your investing goal, experience level, current age, income amount, etc., and it automatically creates your optimum portfolio without you needing to know which stocks and funds to pick for investing your money in, which you can still further tweak of course.

Many financial firms have added robo-advisors to their line of services because of the quick level of service delivery they provide. Some financial companies, for example Charles Schwab, have created hybrid services where robo-advisors are integrated with human wealth managers. Robo-advisor companies include **Wealthfront** (wealthfront.com), **Betterment** (betterment.com), and **M1 Finance** (m1finance.com).

Let's analyze these investment companies:

- **Wealthfront** is one of the most well-known robo-advisors. It is an investment platform specially made for younger folks who wish to invest in mutual funds for their education. Wealthfront collaborates with more than 500 education platforms, which are usually its third party in investments. The minimum amount needed to open an account is $500. Before a portfolio is created, the system will ask you many questions to help the robo-advisor choose the best portfolio for you. Wealthfront will not provide you with investment education because the assumption is that you will trust the system.

- Like Wealthfront, **Betterment** is also geared toward younger adults. It's very similar to Wealthfront, except there is no minimum amount required to open an account. Betterment invests more in bonds than stocks, so it is generally more conservative and therefore safer.

- An interesting investment platform is **M1 Finance**. It is a hybrid of a traditional brokerage and an online robo-advisor. Although it is a fairly new investment platform, it has attracted a lot of investors due to its transparent policymaking and for allowing investors to customize their portfolios. Nevertheless, it does not offer tax-loss harvesting as other investment platforms. The best part about

M1 Finance is that it's easy to use and completely free – unlike Wealthfront and Betterment that both charge a small percentage fee. Those who love or are already using the popular **Robinhood** will love M1 Finance or find it to be an upgraded version of it with the additional bells and whistles, plus being able to buy "**partial shares**" rather than only be restricted to whole shares. *Why do partial shares matter?* If you've ever wanted to owe Amazon stocks (or any expensive stock for that matter) but are to unable to afford the thousand-dollar price tag for one Amazon share – the solution is to buy a portion of **one share**.

To-Do: Find Your Broker

The importance of having a stockbroker is to find one who's right for you. Follow these guidelines:

1. If you know other investors who have brokers, ask them for recommendations. You can also search for

brokers online. However, don't stop there. Contact the **Central Registration Depository** and ask for all materials about your prospective stockbroker. This will also help you review their past records. Also, check the list of investors who are in business with them.

2. Visit the chosen broker and talk to them. Remember that very successful brokers may have enough clients already and may not be looking for new ones. However, as a beginner, you need a broker who will have enough time to assist you.

3. Explain your financial situation and your goals to the broker. Then ask them for their plans that would be beneficial to you. If the broker talks in a simple language that you understand and makes you feel confident without hiding possible risks, that's a good sign you can trust them. Do not forget to ask for their commissions and other fees. It is good to know that there is a kind of broker called "**prop brokerage**." They help the client until he/she starts gaining from the

market. They only take commissions when their clients earn a profit.

Chapter 4:
Building the Foundational Core Understanding

Starting from the Basic

A child trying to learn how to read will have to, first of all, learn about the alphabet followed by the phonetic sound of each letter. These are the fundamentals of the English language.

Every living thing needs food to survive. But that doesn't mean it's easy to prepare and sell food. In fact, food preparation is the hallmark of ingenuity for chefs if they want to survive in the business. Therefore, they train in cooking and catering schools, and also learn how to manage customers and businesses. Cleanliness and health safety are also required in the restaurant business.

Similarly, knowledge in the stock market is indispensable to an investor who wants to make money. In the stock market, stockholders make money depending on their knowledge of the market. It is just like a master chef coming up with a mouthwatering recipe.

So, the stock market has fundamental knowledge that any investor should know before diving headfirst into the market itself. It is easier to understand any topic when you start from the beginning.

Consider this core knowledge a prerequisite to your stock investment endeavor.

The Mechanism of the Market

<u>Real Talk</u>: One **person's loss** in the stock market is another **person's gain**.

That is just how the stock market has been structured. It is a win-lose situation because it is the money lost by one business mogul that will be gained by another. That is why the public will always say that investing in the stock market is a risky deal.

In essence, it obeys the law of conservation of resources. Therefore, anyone going into the market must be a risk-taker…a calculated risk-taker.

For you to understand and win the market, you must know how it operates, what affects its operations and the personnel involved in it. No matter how much you put into the market, without prior knowledge of how it works, you are bound to lose it except with the intervention of a broker.

However, this comes at a cost.

Even if you get the help of a robo-advisor or financial advisor, your level of knowledge in the stock market will determine what questions to ask and how savvy you are in response to changes in the market.

This is the "**X factor**" of how every investor differs from each other – otherwise everybody will be rich in the stock market.

Investor Hierarchy Levels

There are about seven types of investors in the market according to businessman and author Robert Kiyosaki:

a.) **Level-one investors** - These people have nothing to invest. They spend money on everything they see. They live a materialistic life. If they eventually do invest, it will always be at the late hours of the market when real investors are leaving the market. *Guess what?* Level-one investors invest due to greed and they always lose their money to the market.

b.) **Level-two investors** - These folks live very conservative lives. They are savers because they believe that *a penny saved is a penny earned*. They encourage the traditional system of being taken care of by the government. They contribute to 401(k) accounts religiously and always pray that the market doesn't crash. They are ignorant of the market but are fortunate because they have a good broker.

c.) **Smart investors** - This group is mostly made up of educated people who go after financial advisors and seek guidance. They may invest in many different investments. Although they heavily depend on stockbrokers before any decision (even trivial ones), they are better off because they ask a lot of questions and always have something (like good savings) to fall back on.

d.) **Aggressive investors** - These are the bearish and bullish investors. They control the market by venturing into "risky investments." Their fears and greed control the market. An example of an aggressive investor is Warren Buffet

e.) **Capitalists** - These investors set up the companies that eventually register in the stock market to sell their shares. Their activities are what affect the fundamental market analysis. Examples are Elon Musk (Tesla) and Mark Zuckerberg (Facebook).

Where do you belong? The next set of exercises and information is designed to prepare you to become an aggressive investor. People use their intelligence to get money from the stock market at all times. But the next important thing to know is how to interpret every move and predict the future accurately. This involves in-depth knowledge of market analysis.

To-Do: Solidify Investment Goal

1. Write down your financial goals clearly and in simple terms.

2. Write down the reason why you want to start stock trading.

3. Assign a tentative timeline to your short-term and long-term financial goals.

4. Believe it is possible and build a persistent mindset bearing in mind that some level of loss is inevitable.

Chapter 5:

Controlling and Mastering the Stock Market

Honing an Investor's Intuition

Any shrewd investor can make money by using the principles of **pricing and timing**.

- In **pricing**, an investor buys shares lower than their real value and holds them until the stocks appreciate above their real value, and then he sells. This principle demands close attention of the investor to fundamental analysis. This kind of trading is *NOT* for a day trader, but it is much safer and more convenient, especially if the investor does other things to make ends meet.

- In **timing**, the investor sells his stocks when their prices are likely to fall, and buys them when they are likely to rise. Essentially, the investor tries to predict the market and moves in that predictable direction before others.

Here's a simple way to think about it:

Consider the weather. In October, everybody knows that winter is on the way. So, if you're half-smart, you'll plan ahead and make sure you have winter clothes and that your heater works before it gets cold. The exact date of when the cold weather arrives each year will vary. But you still know that winter weather is coming eventually, and you can keep a close eye on the forecast.

Just the same, investors who use timing don't know the exact date when stocks will rise or fall in value, but they will keep a close eye on technical analysis.

Don't forget that what drives the market is **supply and demand**.

> If there are <u>1,000 shares</u> in the market and about <u>10,000 buyers</u> – the price of the stock will go <u>ten times higher</u>. If there are only <u>100 buyers</u> for <u>1,000 shares</u> – then the price will drop <u>ten times lower</u> than the original price. Shrewd investors know when there are limited buyers and buy as much stock as they can afford. Then they wait until that stock is needed in the market. Whenever a stock is needed in the market, there are usually more prospective buyers, so then stockholders sell to the highest bidder.

So to make money in the stock market, you need the intuition to <u>go into the market when others are leaving</u> and leave when others are entering. Thus, understanding human behavior and psyche will help you a long way.

The Driving Polar Forces of the Market

What motivates people or investors to go into the market is the quest to *make money*.

One striking thing about the stock market is that money can be made or lost quickly. To be on the winning curve all the time, you need to pay attention to the psychology catalysts of the market. The two main catalysts are **greed** and **fear**. The reason is tied to human emotions.

These human emotions inspired the terms **bear** and **bull** market.

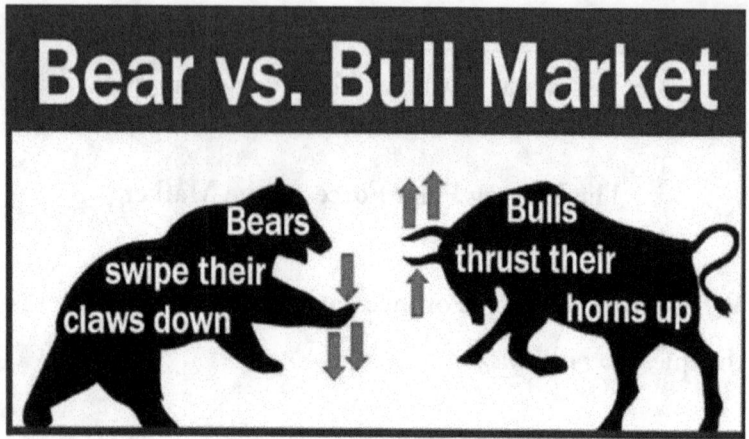

Bull Market: When a bull attacks, it thrusts its horns *up*. So a bull market means stock prices are higher than they were the day before. Obviously, it is when the actual value of a stock is in tandem with traders' opinions and goes even higher. It is caused by many factors. One of them is forecast.

Take this scenario: A Wall Street analyst said on Monday morning that Warren Buffet met Mark Zuckerberg on Friday afternoon with the intention of Buffet buying 10% of Facebook stock. The discussion was *positive*, so the men scheduled another meeting on

Tuesday. The Wall Street analyst predicted that when Buffet buys the stock, he will become a Facebook board member. *What do you think will happen?* Bull market!

Because the analyst predicted a bright future for Facebook, there will be a rush of investors to buy shares of Facebook. *But guess what?* A shrewd investor must have already bought a big chunk of Facebook stock because what attracted his attention to Facebook must have also been what attracted Buffet's attention. *Great minds do think alike!* So when many people will buy due to greed and optimism, the shrewd investor will sell bit by bit of his stock. From this, he may gain up to 1000% of his money and more. In some cases, he may retain part of the stock so that he will still benefit from a long-term investment.

This can also happen if a particular brokerage advised all its clients to invest in Apple stock because their product is becoming even more prominent in the American technology market. If the brokerage has one million clients, and they all bought shares of Apple on Monday morning of the following week, technical analysts and most other investors who study the charts will likely throw in their money.

Bear Market: This is the other side of the stock market coin. When a bear attacks, it swipes its claws *down*. A bear market is driven by fear and pessimism.

Using the same example as in a bull market, after the meeting between Zuckerberg and Buffet, perhaps old Warren told financial reporters that he doesn't expect much from Facebook.

Now what do you think would happen? The price of the stock would go down, and fear will control the stock of the market for the whole week. *Bear market!* The investors who bought high will be forced to sell their stock thereby losing about a percentage of their capital.

In this situation, the shrewd investor who knows the true worth of Facebook stock will buy as much as possible and hold on for the next opportunity, thinking long term.

In essence, a savvy investor understands the market and moves before others do – like a man who decided to spend a relaxing afternoon at the beach. But after a few minutes, he noticed some dark clouds building in the distance. Thinking it might rain, he hopped in his car and drove home. Traffic was light because he noticed the potential for rain before others who were still at the beach when the downpour started. Had the man stayed at the beach until the rain started, he would have gotten wet and then had a longer commute home because everyone else was leaving the beach at the same time.

To be a good investor, you must focus on analyzing the action of the market and anticipating what others might do and not do.

The Art of Stock Analysis

Every investment requires some form of analysis. There are two types of analysis in the stock market: **fundamental analysis** and **technical analysis.**

Fundamental Analysis: This is the foundational knowledge needed in the stock market by any investor to survive. As the name implies, this form of analysis deals with an in-depth search into every detail concerning the company: its management team, its modus operandi, its leadership pattern, how long it has stayed in business, the capital, the number of investors, its brand, the public's opinion about it, its innovations and creativity, and probably its relationship with government in the country where it operates. This will give you an idea of the strength of the company. A company's activities with investors is also a big deal to consider.

- Here's a good example if you can set politics aside for a moment. Let's assume that Donald Trump was a shareholder in Microsoft while he was running for president. That would have boosted the company's value, because people would have predicted that if he won, he would support laws and policies that would favor Microsoft. Although day traders will argue that fundamental analysis is not so important, it forms the bedrock of technical analysis. In fact, Wall Street analysts use fundamental analysis more often than they do with technical analysis.

Technical Analysis: This is a very expensive type of analysis because it takes a great deal of time to understand it (probably <u>six or more</u> months). It is an in-depth study of charts to depict the current trend, and from it predict the future direction of the market. When learned it can help a day investor to be calculative in his dealings in the market.

One of the ways to analyze the market is by reading and understanding the charts.

First, every company trading on the stock exchange does so using a ticker symbol. So when the **company's name** is written, next to the name is the **trading platform** followed by the **ticker symbol**.

For example, Apple trades on the NASDAQ platform, so you will see something like this:

Apple Inc. (NASDAQ: AAPL)

Charts show the directions of the market. At a glance, they help you to understand if a company is growing or regressing. With the in-depth knowledge of the charts, an investor can predict the movement of the market before it happens. As mentioned earlier, staying ahead of the pack is the secret to wealth in stock trading.

We will now be going over some of these different types of charts.

The Candlestick Chart

The market is strongly influenced by the *emotions of the traders*.

A "**candlestick chart**," which started in Japan over a century ago, was designed by Japanese rice merchant Munehisa Homma to show the relationship between the market and the emotions of the traders. This visual representation using different colors makes it easy to understand the market trends at a glance.

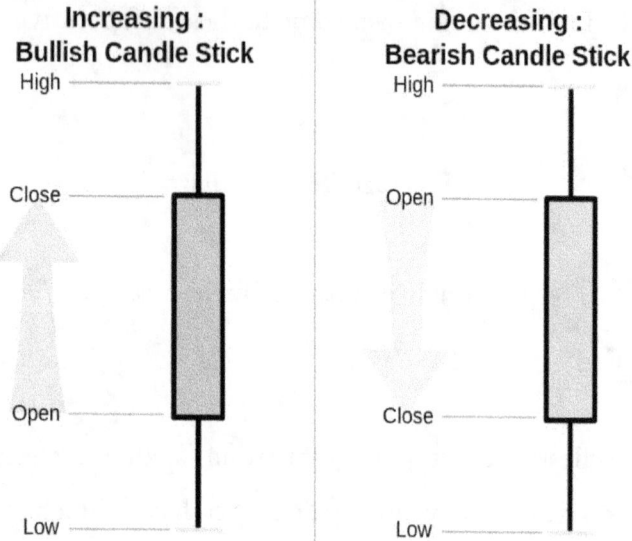

A candlestick is composed of <u>three parts</u>: the **upper shadow, lower shadow,** and **body.** The body is colored green or red. Each candlestick represents a *segmented period of time*. The candlestick data summarizes the executed trades during a specific period of time.

- For example, a five-minute candle represents five minutes of trades data. There are <u>four data points</u> in every candlestick: the **open, high, low,** and **close**.

The **open** is the very *first trade for the specific period* and the **close** is the very *last trade for the period*. The **open** and **close** is considered the body of the candle. The **high** is the *highest priced trade* and **low** is the *lowest price trade for that period*.

The **high** is represented by a *vertical line extending from the top of the body to the highest price* called an "upper shadow" or wick. The **low** of the candle is the "lower shadow" or tail, represented by a *vertical line extending down from the body*.

- If the **close** is *higher* than the **open**, then the body is colored green representing a net price gain (a bullish trend).

- If the **open** is *higher* than the **close**, then the body is colored red as it represents a net price decline (a bearish trend).

The Trendlines Chart

A "**trendline**" is the combination of all candlesticks that shows the *pattern movement of the market* in a minute, hour, day, week or months. This trendline gives the analyst or investor clues about the market.

Here's an example of a trendline chart that shows both a *downward trend* and an *upward trend*.

Does the chart seem a bit confusing to you? Don't worry. Designing and analyzing trend charts may seem a bit intimidating at first. But once you get the hang of it, you'll find it's like riding a bike. You'll never forget.

- Trendlines are better explained when you can visually see how they are supposed to move in action – here's a great video that does that: www.youtube.com/watch?v=n8_1_NUKDAc, or search on YouTube for "How to Draw Charts: Trend Lines for Beginners" by **TheChartGuys**.

The ABCD Chart

Another kind of chart that's good to understand is the "**ABCD chart.**" It is mainly a pattern used by day traders to know the best time of day to buy and sell stocks. It is considered the simplest for the fact that it is also a **risk management technique.**

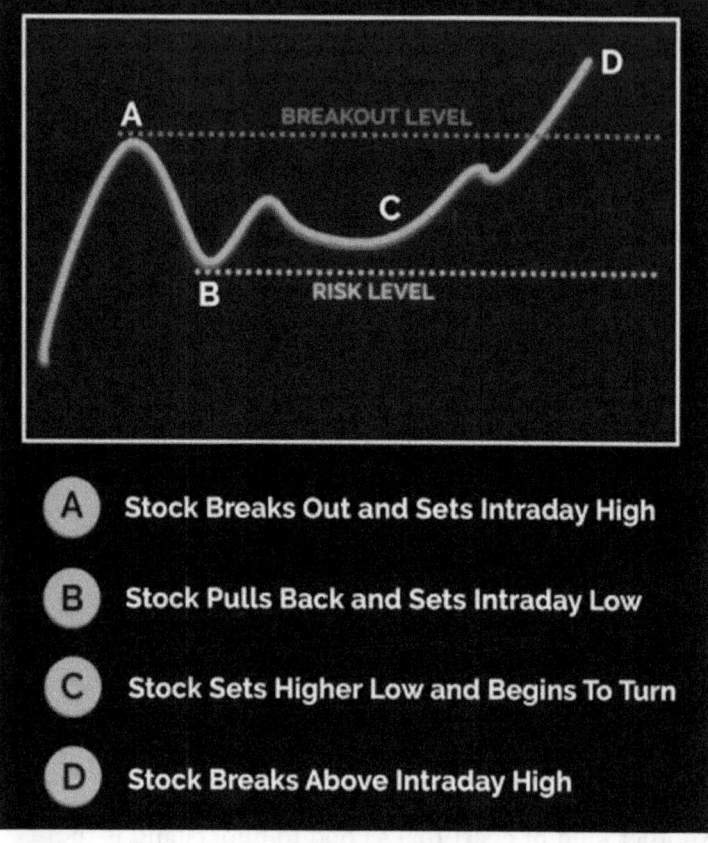

(Point A) - Most traders buy stocks in the morning, perhaps before going to work. That's why you'll see a surge in the market in the morning, which takes the stock to its "open" price.

(Point B) - After the early morning market, there is a reduction of volume, usually until early in the afternoon.

(Point C) - At this point, many investors realize the progress of their stock, and there are also many late investors jumping in who perhaps had been deceived by the early morning price surge. They would want to buy stock now, and bullish traders will be reluctant to sell, making the availability of the stock very low. This causes a kind of tension in the market for a while until around mid-afternoon when the number of buyers seems to exceed that of sellers.

(Point D) - At this point, the price skyrockets until it reaches slightly above D toward the end of the market.

Common Trading Terms

It would be a great idea to know some of these trading terms by heart for their common every trading day usage.

- Open Price: The price of a stock at the beginning of the stock market and at a particular time.

- Close Price: The price of the stock at the end of the market.

- Volume: The number of traders in the market at a time.

- Dollar Volume: The amount of dollars in the market. It is calculated by multiplying the number of shares owned by investors at a time by the stock price value.

- Leverage: A plan to borrow money from a broker in order to execute your business plan. It can be $1 to $100. It means that if you have only $5,000 and want to purchase stock worth $500,000, you only need to notify your broker to lend you money. Although there may be a commission for this, it is far less than the perceived gain.

To-Do: Rubber Meets the Road

Scientists have proven that the best way to learn is not just by watching or reading something but by *actively participating* in it. You can read all the tutorials in the world but still feel overwhelmed. However, as soon as you start taking action, everything will sink in.

1. Sign up for a free **demo account**. Demo accounts mimic the stock market – except that you are not putting in your real money. You practice with *virtual money* meaning that you have nothing to lose. It is called a **"paper trading account."**

- We recommend NinjaTrader, Oanda, and TradingView.

2. The next phase of the process is to download any **Robo-advisor app.** The system will ask you a lot of questions and plot a predictable graph/chart/pie of your financial future for you. It helps to align your actions to suit your goals. Once your portfolio is set to suit your risk level and satisfy your future, your duty is just to check how progressive it is moving toward your goals.

- Our top picks are Betterment, Wealthfront, and M1 Finance.

Chapter 6:

Taking Action and Initiating the Trading Process

Choosing Companies for Personal Portfolio

Like a broken record, it is a good idea to start investing immediately. If you are studious and want to invest, the assumed primary goal is to invest for the long-term future.

For that reason, it is important to invest in **blue chip companies** – or **mid-size S&P companies** – which have the promise of growing rapidly. These are mostly *growth companies* which will take years before they start paying dividends.

Let's assume you make $1,000 per month, and you follow a plan of savings, expenditures, emergency funds, and investing in the ratio of 30:30:30:10. In such a scenario, you would have $100 to invest.

Now, let's assume there are two companies: **Company A** and **Company B**.

Company A is an S&P company, its stock value is $34.70, and its returns in the previous three years were within the range of $3–$5. **Company B** has a stock value of $15, and its returns in the previous three years were within the range of $2–$6. It is advisable to buy stock from **Company B** for the following reasons:

- One, **Company B** looks more volatile for a good investment, and its volatility promises profitable returns because it is a growing stock.

- Two, its stock value is much lower than **Company A**, which means that you can buy more shares from them with just $\underline{\$100}$ than **Company A**. The number of shares bought will determine the amount of dividends you will earn. A dedicated investor can have as high as 50% of his portfolio in stocks. This means that the portfolio may have stocks, bonds, real estate, and index funds in the ratio of 50:20:15:15.

In summary, when you are young and have the luxury of time on your hands, it is a great idea to go for "**growth stocks**" because they have a higher chance of rapid growth. However, they are at a higher risk of liquidation too.

On the other hand, when you are older (probably closer to retirement), you can't afford to take huge risks because you don't have the luxury of time anymore. It is time to be more conservative. Consequently, "**dividend stocks**" will be a better investment option for you. This is because you can be sure that the dividend will keep coming, and they are at a lower risk of liquidation.

Steps to Practice Risk Management

Practice does make perfect. As a new trader, you need to practice a lot to master all you have learned. This is where it is handy to have a **demo account**.

Here, a demo account can give newbies a safe and risk-free platform to execute everything including the *mastery of their emotions*. It is the ideal platform to master your *risk management skill*.

STEP 1: How to create a risk management plan

To start with, never buy a stock that you know nothing about. If you are interested in a particular stock, read and study it. Look at the management team. Check its awards and achievements. Consider the public opinions and ponder the advice of Wall Street analysts on the company of interest. Never rush to buy stock. The stock market has been there for a long time and will continue to be.

If you are confident enough to enter the market, set out a **risk capital** *less than or equal to 3%*.

- Risk capital is defined as "the amount of money that an investor is willing to lose in a market," at which he exits the market.

For example, if you have $10,000 as your main capital for trade in the stock market, in order to get the risk capital, you should multiply the capital by the standard 3%.

3% x $10,000 = $300 *(This is your risk capital.)*

STEP 2: How to determine position sizing

Position sizing is the *number of shares you are willing to buy*. It must be in synchronization to the risk capital which has been set aside.

To get position sizing, you have to consider your *stock of interest*. Using the Coca-Cola Company as an example, having analyzed its management, are you confident that they will push the company forward? You will go to the **New York Stock Exchange (NYSE)** to know the price of the stock and its volatility.

Let's assume it is **$46.75 per share,** and the **volatility is about 0.2%.** You will first multiply that volatility 0.2% by the previous risk capital $300; hence, your position size is:

0.2% x $300 = *500*

The number of shares you can buy is *500 shares*. Therefore, to know the amount to invest in the market, multiply the number of shares by the stock price $46.75:

500 x $46.75 = $23,375

From this calculation, you need $23,375, but you only have $10,000. You need $13,375 more to buy *500 shares* of Coca-Cola stock today.

Therefore, you can use the **power of leverage** to *get the money*. For example, if your broker's leverage ratio is 1:100 then you only need $233.75 to purchase this stock.

STEP 3: How to set your entry and exit point

Entry point is the point *when you bought the shares* and **exit point** is *when you leave the market*.

Every investor wants to leave the market with a bulk of money or the promise of such, but it is not always feasible. It is therefore imperative to know when to leave the market, especially when it is not favorable.

Here, the **risk capital** plays a vital role. Since it is $300 and the number of shares to buy is *500*, you first divide $300 by 500:

$300 ÷ 500 = $0.60 *(Sixty Cents)*

- Your **entry point** will be when the market *is below or equal to* $46.75.

- Your **exit point** will be if the value of the stock value *goes to or below* $46.15. (You get this by s*ubtracting* $0.60 from $46.75.)

- If the value of the stock increases to give you a **profit,** you should exit the market if the price of the stock is *above or equal* to $47.95. (You get this by multiplying $0.60 by *2* and adding that value $1.20 to the initial stock price $46.75.)

To-Do: Calculate Risk Benchmarks

1. If you haven't done so already, open a paper trading account with one of the aforementioned platforms: NinjaTrader, Oanda, and TradingView. Generally,

most of the platforms have a demo account for beginners, and you should always leverage on this to test the waters before throwing in your money.

2. Input the amount of money you would ordinarily use in a real account, for example, $10,000.

3. Create your own formula using the above risk management method. For practice, you can decide to buy shares from Facebook and Coca-Cola once you have read about them and understood their policies. Get 3% of your money ($300). Then divide it into two and follow the formula above.

4. You can get into the real market with real money when you have mastered your emotions.

Cumulative Overview: Five-Action Steps to Take Now!

OK, are you ready to take action? Maybe you've already completed the paper trading process with a demo account, or you're just ready to jump right into real trading. Either way, here's our recommended <u>five-step action plan</u> to get started investing now.

<u>**STEP 1**</u>: Choose your platform. Every platform comes with various pros and cons. Find the one that you're most comfortable with.

For instance, Robinhood and M1 Finance offer free services and are therefore good for newbies who don't have much money to spend on extra charges. Wealthfront and Betterment are also recommended due to their useful online financial advice features, although they take about 0.25-0.40% of your equity. There are many other platforms like Charles Schwab, which can offer full-time financial services and management. This type of service is recommended for those who are financially responsible and comfortable.

RECOMMENDATION:

If you're a BROKE newbie and want everything FREE:

- Start with **Robinhood** and **M1 Finance**.

If you're a FRUGAL newbie and don't mind paying a small percentage fee when you earn money:

- Start with **Betterment** or **Wealthfront**.

If you're an AVERAGE newbie with a standard income and can afford to pay for better services:

- Go with your traditional well-known financial institutions: **Goldman Sachs, Charles Schwab,**

Fidelity, Vanguard, and **Ameritrade**. You'll also have a broker there to talk to if you need to.

(Updated Note: As of *late 2019*, just about every brokerage out there has moved to commission-free, so you can go with any reputable one you want without worrying about paying fees for buying/selling stocks.)

STEP 2: If you have never invested before, start with a RETIREMENT account RIGHT NOW! Draw inspiration and motivation from the previous examples on the power of the compounding effect with the huge difference in returns starting in your 20s and 40s.

What makes the retirement account more powerful over a normal brokerage account is the tax-benefit you'll receive, contrasted to a brokerage account which is heavily taxed.

- We highly recommend the **Roth IRA** because whatever you earn is tax-free and yours to keep. Now some may confuse what a Roth IRA is and assume it is like another bank savings account that automatically earns interest on its own. That's not the case; it's merely a shopping cart to store your chosen investments – that can include stocks, bonds, real estate investment trusts (REITs), and mutual funds that you look forward to appreciate over time and generate great returns.

The first thing that any newbie investor would want to prioritize is to focus on the retirement account; the only drawback is, you can't touch the money without paying a huge financial penalty, so if you need money for a rainy day now – this isn't really a suitable option.

STEP 3: After you have opened your RETIREMENT account or if you already had one, it is time to open a regular BROKERAGE account. You may be tempted to ask, *"Why not open more RETIREMENT accounts instead of a BROKERAGE account?"*

The answer is simple: There's a legal limit to how much you can contribute to an IRA each year (currently $6,000 starting in 2019 from the previous $5,500 yearly maximum contribution). A BROKERAGE account has no limit, and you can liquate that whenever you want – meaning you can sell your shares whenever for spending cash.

STEP 4: *What do you put in your account?* Start with having an ETF, either any **S&P 500 ETF**, **Total Market ETF**, or **World Market ETF**. *Why?* Let's review the S&P 500 one last time to drive it all home.

> The great thing about going with an ETF stock like one of the S&P 500 ETFs – such as ticket symbols <u>VOO</u> (**Vanguard S&P 500 ETF**), <u>VTI</u> (**iShares Core S&P 500 ETF**), and <u>SPY</u> (**SPDR S&P 500 ETF**) – is because it consists of the "500 BEST performing companies" combined into one fund. If one company all of a sudden slips and performs badly or goes bankrupt, that <u>one</u> defunct company (out of the <u>500</u> companies) will be switched out with another company, maintaining its market performance. It's almost like a foolproof way to prevent you from losing money (because the idea of all 500 top companies going bankrupt simultaneously is unheard of).
>
> *Want more proof?* Based upon history of the market, it tends to appreciate over time, even though there will be

downturns of a bear market (which is the best time to buy). But overall, the average of the market tends to go up as can be seen by the S&P 500 historical performance chart, again being the common assessment of the market (www.macrotrends.net/2324/sp-500-historical-chart-data).

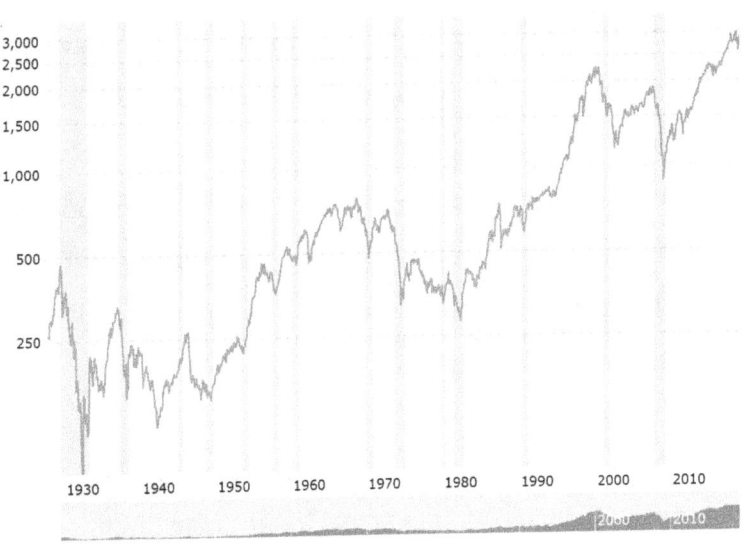

If during recessions and periods of financial downturn (like the Great Depression between 1929-1939 and the 2008 financial crisis) people are patient and hold on to their investment, they would still make money. Many people fear investing due to the perception of losing money – thanks to the constant talk about downturn and a bear market. To any savvy investor, what's one's loss is another's opportunity; they're crafty enough to know how to utilize the bad situation into their advantage – which counterintuitively, they buy more during a bear market. The important thing is to always have the long-term in sight. Yes, the stock will fall, but broadly speaking, the stock market goes up even after a drop or recession. To put it bluntly, the market (S&P 500) has always bounced back, unlike a company stock that can be hot for one day but goes bankrupt and disappears the next.

*What about **Total Market ETFs** and **World Market ETFs?*** A Total Market ETF comprises all U.S. companies (not only the 500 best U.S. companies), and the World Market ETF is all of the U.S. companies *PLUS* international companies. Their performances are essentially similar to the S&P 500 but *slightly more* *diversified*. The S&P 500 just has a *longest proven track record* (without possible dead weight from weaker performing companies), regardless of how the reward can be small and slow at times but ideal for long-term investing.

After adding an ETF (preferably any of the S&P 500), then add some governmental bonds because these are the safest investments out there in case something happens, these bonds will balance the loss. Slowly as you gain more confidence, experience, and wisdom – add the stocks you like and optimize your portfolio over time.

STEP 5: Continue to add more funds and reinvest the dividends for the long-term compounding effect, and allow it to passively sit and make you money.

Overall, investing in the stock market can get overwhelming with all the things you need to know, but follow these five steps and you should be in good hands.

Chapter 7:

The Prosperous Final Outlook for Financial Future

A Renewed Financial Affair

The business of buying or selling in the stock market does not require you to be exceptionally brilliant or a genius. Anyone can do it – *including you!* It just requires the act of discipline and determination. "Optimistic scrutiny" should be the watchword of every investor because a *penny lost by one investor* is a *penny gained by another*.

Start small and grow your portfolio when your feet are strong enough to go deeper into this murky water called "stock."

One wise piece of advice you should take if you are diving into stocks as a newbie is – past performance doesn't always correlate with future price. For example, if Apple hits $130 per share yesterday, that doesn't mean it will do so again today. Likewise, this doesn't mean it can't hit $260 tomorrow.

The bottom line is that there is no way to tell. Never allocate more than 10% of your portfolio to individual stock picking. Therefore, it is often a good idea to start by focusing on index funds and bonds while you figure out the stock market.

Also, learn the market strategies with patience and meticulousness. Understand the ins and outs of the candlestick. Sitting in front of your computer all day watching the trendlines does not guarantee success. Study the movement of population and try to outsmart them. Do not be afraid to fail in stocks, but do not let the greed of getting more from the market push you away from your financial plan. Maintaining your risk management plan is important to minimize your losses in the case of eventualities.

Mistakes will definitely happen along the way, but they will also provide you learning opportunities. Diligence only requires you to be scrupulous enough with your emotions and portfolio to minimize your risk or loss. If you can control your greed and anxiety, you will control your loss, as well as the market and not let it control you.

Fear Not the Loss of Money but of Time

The biggest takeaway we hope you have gained is a change in mindset to approach the stock market for the long term and to not let pessimism rule you when the market goes down. Just like the market will go down, it will also bounce right back up and that will be the time that you will be glad that you had held on for profit. You can always take advantage of the market regardless of an upturn or downturn period by selling high during a bull market and buying low during a bear market.

What we are trying to say is – any fear in the *loss of money* from investing is trivial compared to the *loss of time* that is already losing you money from not investing.

If you have meticulously followed all that you have learned up to this point, you will discover that one thing is clear: the earlier you start investing in stocks, the better. To enjoy the cumulative compounding nature of stock investing, the best time to start is now. Every day that goes by slims your chances of maximizing this benefit. If you are already in your thirties then you should be planning for your retirement already.

Inasmuch as you need to learn as much as possible about stock trading, you don't have to keep waiting to become an expert before you start trading. In the real sense, no one is truly an expert. Even the so-called "experts" lose money once in a while. Again, those who have attained the level of being called "masters" did not get there overnight. It took them many years of practice to get there. Practice until you become perfect!

But by all means…start investing <u>now</u> rather than piling cash under your pillow or allowing it to lie dormant in your bank account!

www.ingramcontent.com/pod-product-compliance
Lightning Source LLC
Chambersburg PA
CBHW070659220526
45466CB00001B/500